Flightpaths

Caitlin Press Inc.
8100 Alderwood Road,
Halfmoon Bay, BC V0N 1Y1
www.caitlin-press.com

Text and cover design by Vici Johnstone
Cover art by Linda Gass ©, cover art photographed by Don Tuttle
Printed in Canada

Caitlin Press Inc. acknowledges financial support from the Government of
Canada and the Canada Council for the Arts, and the Province of British
Columbia through the British Columbia Arts Council and the Book Publisher's
Tax Credit.

Library and Archives Canada Cataloguing in Publication

Greco, Heidi, author
    Flightpaths : the lost journals of Amelia Earhart / Heidi Greco.

Poems.
ISBN 978-1-987915-47-1 (softcover)

    1. Earhart, Amelia, 1897-1937—Poetry. I. Title.

PS8563.R41452F55 2017   C811'.6   C2017-901989-9

Flightpaths

The Lost Journals of Amelia Earhart

HEIDI GRECO

CAITLIN PRESS

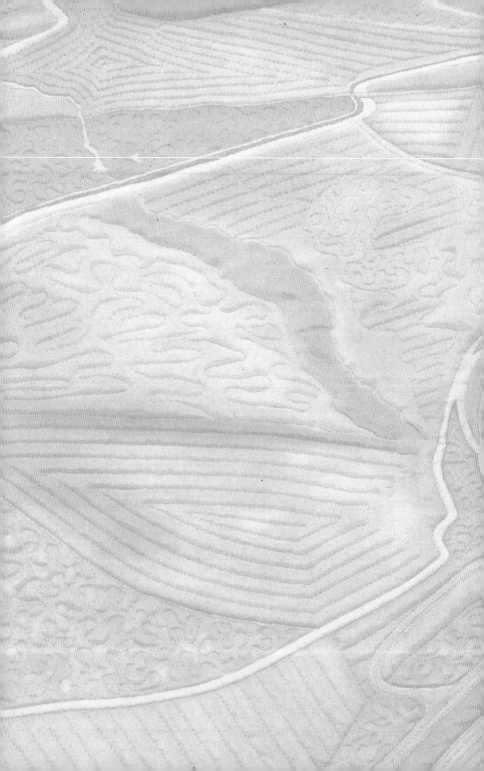

Dedicated to the memory of Bessie Coleman, who, but for circumstance, might have become the first woman to fly around the world — and for Amy (Johnnie) Johnson, another explorer of the air — and, of course, for Ann Pellegreno, who did it.

With gratitude to Louise Foudray, the keeper.

Contents

Notes

Readers will find, throughout the various notebook jottings, some variant spellings (e.g., okeh, cocoanuts). These are true to the era and can be found in actual letters that were written by Earhart.

Page 33: "Grace, in Newfoundland" reconstructs a memory of Earhart's transatlantic solo in 1932. Departing for Paris exactly five years after Lindbergh's flight, she chose Newfoundland (not yet part of Canada) as her departure point for its relative proximity to Europe. Off-course, she landed in a farmer's pasture in Ireland — not Paris, but safely across the Atlantic and into the record books.

Page 36: James the Ferocious was Amelia's beloved dog, whose death was a huge emotional blow, coming at a time when her parents' marriage was going through one of its many difficult spells. Amelia was sure her pet had been poisoned by a cruel man who lived a few houses away from her grandparents' home in Atchison. The quoted words are attributed to Earhart.

Page 40: "For Pidge, an Afternoon at the Fair" contains a phrase credited to Amelia Earhart. When she first saw a plane in flight at the State Fair in Iowa, she is said to have called it "a thing of rusty wire and wood. "

Page 41: The woman referred to in "Reminiscent of Eleanor" is Eleanor Roosevelt, then First Lady of the US.

Page 43: July 13's entry mentions the letter of agreement that Earhart insisted George Putnam sign before their wedding. It specified that monogamous faithfulness was not required and also that should either one wish, the marriage could be dissolved after the span of one year.

Page 56: The series called "from the dirt yard" has had numbers inserted to distinguish the entries from each other. These may not be the order in which they were written. The "skinny birds who cannot fly" in "from the dirt yard [3]" are most likely a type of flightless rails known to have inhabited small islands in the southern Pacific, and quite possibly one of the species that became extinct about the middle of the twentieth century.

Page 61: The entry for July 18 contains a reference to Ellie and Donk. These were beloved playthings of Amelia and her sister — jointed wooden animals, an elephant and a donkey.

Page 70: Druid Hill Park is one of the oldest parks in Baltimore. Centrally located, it may have been a site a displaced Earhart would have visited.

Page 86: There is evidence that in the 1930s Arthur "Harpo" Marx served as a courier carrying messages between Russia and the US.

Page 87: The letter to her father is sheer fancy. Earhart's wedding took place in 1931, and her father died in 1930. Nonetheless, it is an example of Amelia's love of wordplay at its punniest, written in the almost-secret language she often used in letters to her father.

Page 91: The Swiss Federal Institute of Technology, referred to in the transcript cited in "Postscript," was founded in 1854. Among its prestigious graduates was Albert Einstein.

Amelia Earhart got in her plane
early one morning in May.
We followed her journey around the world
but then she just flew away.

[Fragment, skipping-rope chant, c. 1938]

Amelia Earhart was born on July 24, 1897, in an upstairs bedroom at her maternal grandparents' home in Atchison, Kansas. The house overlooks the Missouri River and was, from all accounts, the happiest place Amelia ever lived. She and her sister Muriel ("Pidge") played rough-and-tumble games there. They even built a kid-sized roller coaster in the Atchison backyard — a device on which Amelia got her first taste of an experience that felt to her "like flying."

Once she got a taste for the actual experience of flight, she committed herself to it and to accomplishing feats not considered acceptable for women. Oddly, though she was technically the first woman to fly across the Atlantic, she had to do so as a passenger — or, as she put it, as "a sack of potatoes on a wooden box."

Soon after, she was able to take on a more active role, thanks in part to her being "discovered" by the book publisher George Palmer Putnam ("GP"), whom she married in 1931. Working with her slight resemblance to the famous pilot Charles Lindbergh, she was dubbed "Lady Lindy" and made to play out a role as a very public figure. She may well have been the first consciously created celebrity, criss-crossing the country and making appearances for which she was well paid. Through profits from these events and through product endorsements (a brand of luggage and a fashion line both bore her name — other less judicious choices, such as Lucky Strike cigarettes, also claimed her), she accrued funds for the flights that would bring her even greater fame.

A role model for many, Earhart was a feminist, a pacifist, an author and a very creative person. Even as a child she loved word games and puns. Later, she wrote poetry. Some poems were published, though most were lost in a fire that destroyed the home in Rye, New York, that she shared with Putnam.

Her accomplishments were many — first woman to fly solo across the Atlantic, first woman to fly coast to coast across the US, first woman to receive the Distinguished Flying Cross. Regrettably, the feat that seems to have bestowed her most enduring fame is her disappearance.

Last seen taking off from Lae, Papua New Guinea, on July 2, 1937, Amelia was only a few weeks shy of her fortieth birthday. She was accompanied by her navigator, Fred Noonan, and the flight plan had them heading for the tiny Howland Island, where the US had constructed a landing strip. This was a key leg in her effort to be the first person — woman or man — to fly around the world at the equator. It was also the most treacherous portion of the flight, as it was over a vast tract of open sea. Strange as it seems, some believe that Earhart may not have been in the plane that was the subject of the intensive search, as there have been reports of an identical craft parked near the runway at Lae, complete with a stand-in as its pilot.

The situations presented in these journals explore variations on several of the many explanations regarding her final outcome. Over the years, I consulted sources that ranged from books to personal interviews and of course Internet sites, including Wikipedia. Grounded in facts, the pieces in this book fly on wings of imagination, speculating what might have become of the famous pilot Amelia Earhart. Although some outcomes may seem improbable, it is impossible to deny the possibility of any of them being true.

Despite extensive searches (some going on even today), no definitive trace of her has yet been found.

Departure city	Arrival city	Distance nautical miles	Notes
Oakland, California	Burbank, California	283	Off to a great start!
Burbank	Tucson, Arizona	393	
Tucson	New Orleans, Louisiana	1070	
New Orleans	Miami, Florida	586	Final servicing of plane
Miami	San Juan, Puerto Rico	908	Over water, looks so big and wet
San Juan	Caripito, Venezuela	492	Out of Isla Grande Airport
Caripito	Paramaribo, Surinam	610	
Paramaribo	Fortaleza, Brazil	1142	
Fortaleza	Natal, Brazil	235	
Natal	Saint-Louis, Senegal	1727	Transatlantic leg, over 13 hours
Saint-Louis	Dakar, Senegal	100	
Dakar	Gao, French Sudan	1016	
Gao	Fort-Lamy, FE Africa	910	
Fort-Lamy	El Fasher, Anglo-Egyptian Sudan	610	
El Fasher	Khartoum, Anglo-Egyptian Sudan	437	
Khartoum	Massawa, Ethiopia	400	
Massawa	Assab, Italian Eritrea	241	
Assab	Karachi, British India	1627	First ever non-stop flight from Africa to India!
Karachi	Calcutta, British India	1178	
Calcutta	Akyab, Burma	291	
Akyab	Rangoon, Burma	268	
Rangoon	Bangkok, Siam	315	
Bangkok	Singapore, Straits Settlements	780	

Singapore	Bandoeng, Dutch East Indies	541	
Bandoeng	Soerabaja, Dutch East Indies	310	Delayed here by monsoon
Soerabaja	Bandoeng, Dutch East Indies	310	Returned for repairs to plane and to me (dysentery)
Bandoeng	Soerabaja, Dutch East Indies	310	
Soerabaja	Koepang, Dutch East Indies	668	
Koepang	Darwin, Australia	445	Direction finder repaired, parachutes sent home
Darwin	Lae, New Guinea	1012	
Lae	Howland Island	2224* 2556	[Did not arrive]
Howland Island	Honolulu, Hawaii	1900*	[Projected only]
Honolulu	Oakland, California	2090*	[Projected only]

* Sources vary regarding projected distances.

Dead Reckoning
July 2 and 2, crossing the dateline

Last night's half-moon might have been a sign
her sly grin chiding my defiance of the gods,
daring to ring the globe in my Electra, metal bird,
bold enough to greet the morning sun.

Later, when the long mouth of darkness closed on us,
swallowing the guiding constellations,
still we stayed our course, hoping for a glimpse
Polaris or the Southern Cross to indicate the way.

Howland, tiny island, how to land
on a hummingbird's nest.

After the rising peach of dawn
profiled against Earth's curve,
sea and sky merge seamless, a curtain of blue on blue.

Twenty hours, plenty hours, and I can no longer see
the line distinguishing ocean from heavens above.

Horizon is but a memory, vision from when I believed
I could be first to accomplish this flight, swinging wide
across these open tracts of vacant sea. Perhaps

my doubts are merely lack of sleep or dwindling fuel,
rather than weakness of mind or will.

I startle each time small wrinkles reveal
some briefest definition: which way reflection,
above or below.

A frilling of white, that's all I need,
breakers against some point of land.

How-land, tiny island, how to find land.
Howland, how to land
where I can see no land.

July 3

Today we should have been off to Honolulu. There we would have endured ceremonies, had leis festooned around our necks, long enough for the photographers to have their pound of flash. Instead we are here, some nowhere of a place. Emergency rations are tasteless but okeh. Three canteens of water remain. Fred had half a sandwich in the pocket of his jacket, which he insisted I take for my breakfast. With radio still working, all is well. Surely the waiting Navy ships will fix on our signal and be here soon. If only I can clear my mind of how the plane groaned, creaking protests as she bent in angles unintended. My fears of drowning rose up unbidden, like a brook swelling after spring rains — the sweep of water across the window's glass — rising, rising.

Crashed

"Mayday, mayday, SOS.
This is KHAQQ.
Earhart and Noonan here.
Over."

How many times did I make the call,
sending and sending
an echo of myself.

So much for finding Howland
silly pimple on the sea, downed
instead on fortunate rock
and narrowest strip of sand.

We saw the shift in color,
necklace of reef in ocean.
Knew we had to aim for
the shallows near the beach.

We dragged each other from the Electra,
her shoreward wing bent to a V.
Teetering, she straddles the lip of the reef,
fuselage tipped like some wallowing beast
already half-filled with water.

My ankle bent inward, not good for much.
Fred (with a spearing of metal
somewhere deep in his gut) keeps asking
for his flask of hootch, knowing this time
I will say nothing.

At least, kind friend, he'd grabbed his 'chute
(should have been dumped back in Darwin,
less weight). For this slight betrayal, the refuge
it will provide, I am grateful.

Meanwhile, I keep sending "Mayday,
mayday, SOS, Earhart and Noonan."

Messages lost as the faintest cry
of a frigate bird skimming
the crest of waves.

4th of July, barely there atoll

This was to be our day of celebration, California our final destination. I console myself thinking instead how folks in Atchison will gather in front of my grandparents' house. They'll sprawl in sweet grass on the riverbank while fireworks fill the summer sky. With the moon waning, the stars here grow in intensity, so tonight they will serve as my private fireworks. If only I could interest poor Fred in watching with me. He could tell me the names of the stars and I would make stories to go along with them. He has always loved the sky, has let the constellations guide him. This time they might only lead him to the heavens. He will probably rest while I look for falling stars, making fervent wishes as I watch my homemade fireworks, glittering for a party of one.

By the dawn's early light

Two knives but no flint
to spark light against the dark.

Fred's book of matches
bleeds a soggy pink, alongside
the Unlucky Strikes tucked in his sock
navy man's trick gone awry.

If only the blazing heat of day
could be packed up for night
opened as a welcome lamp
at the twilight's last gleaming.

Oh, for the glow of a fire to warm us,
throw its comfort and joy.

July 5

In pictures I drew as a child in Kansas, I colored the ocean blue. But this expanse before me has moods as fickle as those of some sassy brat. Every time I look, its tone and face have shifted — from gray to green to nearly black, from smooth to rippled or ruffled in white. These variations bring relief from boredom, though sometimes they cause me alarm, when it appears the sea might rise high enough to submerge us. But I like the suddenness of sunsets. Getting used to the long arm of night that descends and chills us so quickly. I take comfort in the canopy of the swirling Milky Way, its stars beyond counting. This is no postcard desert island, to be sure — no palms with cocoanuts — still, a spit of land. One thing unmoving in this constantly moving god-forsaken water.

Course Correction

I fear we are farther south than planned
two vagabonds astray,
riding the belt of the Equator.

Caring for Fred more difficult
than my tending flying aces
in Toronto years ago, that terrible war.
No supplies to ease him, the fright of his pain.

Grateful for this morning's breeze
the mercy of its camouflage:
the stench of his wound that grows
more dread-full each day.

I have taken to singing to him,
"Pennies from Heaven" today,
shifting the words, clowning around,
trying to make him smile.

Cupcakes from heaven, cookies from heaven,
cornbread and fried eggs, divine —
warbling scrumptiously off-key.
Fred croaking back, Hot Dogs. Heaven.

This morning I sang to the radio,
hoping my music would reach someone
thinking that whistled notes might fly
farther aloft than words.

Maybe as far as Florida, New Orleans, Tennessee,
or reaching the barren heat, red dirt Australia.
A girl with her head bent, straining to hear
words from her crystal set, behind the staticky buzz.

July 6

Each day's tides claw their way slightly higher across the sand. The rising waters may ruin my chance at the radio, or even take the plane, already nearly immersed. I have scrounged as much as I can, foraging for supplies when the tide ebbs. Even then, it is difficult. This morning I tripped, grazed my bent ankle on a rock so sharp it drew blood. The salt stung so I howled a stream of swears. Did my best to console myself with minor booty. The tin of graham crackers, broken to pieces but okeh. Batteries in a pocket flashlight, swollen with wet. Neither drying them in the sun nor scraping has restored them. But also a treasure, the First Aid kit. Mercurochrome cracked open, bled orange into bandages which may still be of use. And, hallelujah, a stoppered bottle I think might be morphine! The label too blurred for me to be sure, but they are worth trying on Noonan. I curse not finding the flare guns, but at least I rescued my stock of tomato juice. I've craved its salty tang. Finally, some nourishment Fred is able to swallow. By tonight's high tide I will know whether the pills bring him any relief.

July 7

Too many days without any sign. No rumbled sound of engine, no metal glint from sun. Not so much as a drizzled wisp of smoke on the horizon. I am starting to lose faith and wonder, is anyone looking? The pills seem to have helped poor Noonan (at least he sleeps, holds the parachute tightly to his chin, teeth a-chatter even in noonday sun). I've got more than a hunch that he is dying and have started shallowing out a grave. The salt grass pulls out in easy clumps, the start of a hole. I bet I look like a badger, pushing the sand aside, willing it not to fall back in. All of this out of sight from where he lies shivering. I hope it will not be too far for me to move him.

Cipher

Zero by 180: coordinates any fool could find.
Even me. Or Noonan at his very worst
stone drunk.

Our plane with its netted-up ping-pong balls
meant to provide flotation,
we made it to shore, then waited.

Some day I might learn about
the party sent to find us.
No doubt the biggest in history.

Countless ships and planes engaged
in search of an enemy.

Our gal Amelia the public excuse
as they scatter across the sea
in headlines blackened with lies.

Convoys combing waves
for the needle they had planted
in a haystack they'd quietly
      agreed to move.

July 8

Made an awkward wade to the plane, for another quick series of maydays. Dumb luck revealed a little sack of fruit floating beside my seat (how could I have missed it?), a gift from one of the sweet women at Lae. She'd handed it over smiling, saying repeatedly, "po po." She should have said "poo poo" as it's not agreed with me. Shit, shat, shatted. Enormously. I may have lost more fluids than the soggy fruit supplied. Modesty long gone between Noonan and me. Even so, this is beyond normal, requires some privacy. Glad again that I ripped apart my trousers, creating more of a skirt. Eleanor and Katharine, my cohorts in independence, would laugh at how ladylike I've become.

Shopping with Hepburn

We're in cahoots, out on the town,
looking for deals and raising Cain.

If only she could resist
mocking what she calls my twang,
braying at my loosened vowels, the slur
of blurry consonants refusing to be crisp.
(I can't help if I was born in Kansas.)

If only these shop-girls would stop
their elbow jabs, rolling their eyes, sighing
at our every request: something simpler,
straighter of line, no doodads or ruffled frills —
or, as Kate intones in her Bostony French,
"sans decoration, s'il vous plait."

If only she'd stop
half-shouting at them, as if
that would make our desires
any plainer.

If only we could stop
laughing like monkeys
a pair who like to wear
the pants in the family.

July 9

Alas, this morning's sea is smooth, the horizon uninterrupted, the plane no longer visible. No more surprise supplies for Fred and me, but worse, no radio. Our reliable Electra must have tumbled over the reef in last night's winds. We're just lucky we weren't washed away too. The waters crashed near enough to splash, leaving us miserably wet. To top things off, once the waters eased, the sand pricked for hours, making sleep impossible. And now the heat is merciless, with distant growling thunder. Drum rolls for this ongoing drama of ours.

Grace, in Newfoundland

That was the place I first stepped off the earth,
got lost on my way to Paris, still learning then
about being alone, about the vastness of sea.

Standing in the wind that day,
I touched my foot to an upturned rock
jutting from the spine of the bony field.

A momentary stepping-stone, it granted small pause,
as if charging me to find its mate
across, on the opposite shore.

With a gifted thermos of homemade soup tucked beneath my arm,
I ducked into the cockpit, smiling and waving —
then revved the engine, gritted my teeth and took off.

Circling up and over the bay
into the mouth of the wind,
icebergs swirled below, a white flotilla.

Onward and over the rage of Atlantic
its face a snarling tangle of spit and waves.

My foe today the endless Pacific,
where I may again take a step off the earth,
only this time, forever.

July 10

This morning Fred was cold, the slippery parachute wrapping him, the shroud it was destined to be. With guilty hands, I untangled the silk, brown from days and nights of sand and honestly, who-knows-what. Despite its grime, I trust that it will protect me from winds that howl here, shelter me through the long bouts of darkness. I buried his book along with him. Unlike mine, his filled only with numbers, inscrutable calculations. Maybe some coded prayer to a god all his own.

Noonan, RIP

Beach soil settles quickly.
The little mound he lies beneath

barely visible now, only
this morning I laid him there.

My tears and feeble words
stand as his only marker.

So he tippled the bottle.
None of that matters now.

He deserves much more
than a pile of windswept sand.

Remembering James the Ferocious, poisoned

At least he had a headstone of sorts,
a shiny penny to mark his death, 1907.

I buried him ten paces south
of the sycamore tree down the road,

pronounced a brave eulogy for my dear pet:
"Not just a mere dog.

More a man than the one
who murdered him."

July 11

This island now emptier than my dwindled store of hope, departed along with Fred for more promising shores. I am sore marooned. Only the insects remain. They have discovered the continent of me. Judging from the bites everywhere, I guess I am delicious. I suppose they've swarmed from beneath the grasses I yanked out for his grave. At least he was spared this particular torment. The salt water soothes me, dulling the itch. Perhaps that silly beauty cream in my bag will be of some use after all. Complications upon complications.

Dr. Berry's Ointment

that ridiculous jar of freckle cream
a last-minute gift from GP

yet another something to erase me

make me into who he wanted
me to be

July 12

To think I used to mope about the thickness of my ankles, call them my elephant legs. Bigger than ever the ankle is blooming, like an overfed dahlia in my cousin's flower bed. Now it truly holds the shape of an elephant's leg, would make a good umbrella stand for someone's elegant foyer. Yet despite its bulbous shape, it feels as if the bones are disintegrating. As if the constant salt air has seeped inside and begun dissolving them. Can't distract myself from the pain anymore. Reciting poems, making up songs, repeating my times tables, nothing does the trick. Zero times 180 is still zero. Since Fred no longer needs the pills, I may try using the ones that remain. What effect they may have on me, I cannot say. Tomorrow I mean to begin some letters to family and friends. Perhaps a batch of sweet fare-thee-wells.

For Pidge, an Afternoon at the Fair

All I wanted that day was our father
to buy ice creams for us
let us ride the Ferris wheel
its round and round again

not for him to point and shout
about the noisy aeroplane
wobbling back and forth
across the summer sky.

To me, it was only annoying,
a thing of rusty wire and wood
sputtering terrible sounds, awkward,
some prehistoric bird.

All I wanted was our father
between us, holding our hands.

Reminiscent of Eleanor

This morning I woke to a pink bouquet,
your toes pressed against my cheek, maybe
some tiny imprints there. Hard to resist tickling.

Instead, I bless them with
a row of wake-up kisses,
then rise from the bed to make your hot tea,
open the blinds to morning light.

Sprawled atop the folds of quilt, you're still
in your gown from the masquerade ball.
An errant feather from your mask floats to the fold of your ear,
strands of pearls fly loops in your silvering ringlets of hair,
precious beads shining white on white.

Later, I will whisk you to the edge of the airfield
take you for another of our secret flights and ask:
put on last night's archéd mask, flick your poufy feathers at me.
Then you'll giggle when I don my serious goggles.

How I adore your intake of breath when I pull back on the stick,
the glow on your face when we're high above the world
    no one
    but you and I and sky.

GP and me: Our story

He said he'd buy me a plane.
First thing he vowed.
He said he'd buy me a plane.
        Let me paint it yellow.

He said he'd buy me a plane. Just
        wanted me to play
        at being Lady Lindbergh, fly
        hard and high as I could dream.

He said he'd buy me a plane.
        All I had to do
        was be his bride
        his lucky charm.

He said he'd buy me a plane.
        All I had to do
        was say I do, I do.
        All I had to do just
        Do be do be do.

July 13

Well, I haven't written letters, only chased a few memories. Those at least pour forth, bring me both comfort and guilt. I can hardly admit how spoiled I've been. GP has helped me gain so much, and in return I have grown so self-centered. He can never know the betrayals I have withheld from him, though I expect he likely has a few of his own up his sleeve. The weight of that note of promise when we wed continues to press on me. One year to give it our best shot. One year only. One year years ago. Something more to rue.

All those photo sessions

GP couldn't fathom my reluctance to pose,
my distaste at allowing the painting of pancake
powders and pencil lines. So many days I closed my lips quiet,

complied so my teeth wouldn't show, then smiled
around the tomboy gap, the gap that kept growing
within my lonesome heart.

I still detest that portrait of me:
air-brushed in pilot's helmet (ivory silk no less)
as if I am a film star, some modern Pearl White.

Perhaps that's what he loved: could picture me, black and white,
bound to narrowing tracks in a flickery silent film,
wisps of hairdo a-ruffle in evening breeze.

The locomotive nearing, its throaty whistle screams
while clouds of huffing steam enlarge the screen with danger,
he sees himself — mustachioed hero — swooping in to save me.

He must have never known Pearl White chose to have no stand-in
managed those urgent rescues, precarious stunts all on her own,
just as I know that I too will probably need to do.

July 14

Today is the day of the Bastille Rebellion, with grumbling of thunder all day. Heat lightning as dusk falls along the horizon, a surrogate celebration, long live liberty. How is it I remember a date such as this, yet never anyone's birthday but my own? Darkness around me so soon. I need to keep fiddling, but have almost worked out a way to catch more rain. Remembering the old barrel in Kansas. Bent an empty juice tin to make a kind of eave that will feed my water jug. Surface area, always the key.

Cloudlist

Wispy. Pidge's hairs entangled in my brush.

Streaky. Marks from a Crayola polishing our coaster tracks.

Straggly. Fishbones from a cartoon swimming across the sky.

Wrinkly. Aunt Rilla's sheets, fresh from the line, smelling of sunlight.

Fluffy. Sandburg's slow-moving little cat feet.

Cottony. Dainty enough for my grandmother's vanity.

Billowy. Creamy breasts pillowing, delicious white curves.

Lumpy. Mashed potatoes. Thanksgiving with Mother and Father, together.

Grumpy. Uncle Nicey's cheeks puffed out, harrumphing at the news.

Cloudless. Utter blue.

July 15

No rain, only thunder. Rumblings of guilt. Was it just my pride that made me think I could make this flight? Was it truly that important to do what no one else had done? Maybe it was a bad idea, that membership in the Navy. What did those men in Washington really want from me? Strings attached, tangled, as a miscaught round in a game of cat's cradle. Should I ask GP (will I ever see him again?) about that other plane Fred and I saw at Lae? Was it there simply for parts? Or is there another Amelia in the wings?? In the wings, ha-ha! If there is, GP, will you find her, make her famous too? For my sake, dearest man, please don't. Fame simply ain't all it's cracked up to be. Or maybe it's just me that's cracking up.

"Step right up, little lady"

tired of how these men
doh-see-doh me round the tarmac
squeezing timid smiles from me
flirting for a kiss

I suspect they dream
of pushing buttons, twirling dials
grabbing throttles, shoving
hard between my legs

think of how they'd love
for me to dip a wing and tumble
crash and burn, scattering parts
across some stubbled field

I bet they'd gather their cronies,
tell them they had clutched me
felt my woman's heart
a-flutter

July 16

Took two of Fred's pills. Mistake? Already, everything is fuzzing, my fingertips are numb. Half-moon is in shadow. Partly blocked by puffs of cloud too light for rain, shapes like so many piggy-wigs snuffling. Thought I heard an engine. Thought I saw a glint of light reflect from the Electra, but then I remembered she's gone gone gone deep beneath the waves. Or maybe back to sky where she belongs. A ditty for her.

Tiptoe
through the rosies
lovely poseys
come and follow me
and tiptoe
through the rosies
with me.

Invisible woman pilot

Fred and I watched without a word
as that other Electra lifted off
climbed above morning's rising mist,
then vanished.

Only then did we clamber aboard
settle for our suspect flight
secret disappearing act
all our own.

All of us wear our deceptions
safe and close to the heart
a locket with a photograph
near where the wishbone lies.

July 17

The pill eased the pain in my leg, but played tricks with my mind. Still, sleep was such a relief after the nights I've spent tossing on the sand, measuring stars as they pass overhead, their rolling constellations. Although the drug has left my mouth drier than before, I don't care. I will take another tablet tonight, even if it means more strange dreams. I've tried to go easy on the water. Admittedly, it goes further without sharing sips with Fred, but I need rain soon. At least there is thunder growing in the distance. Maybe this time its rumbling will bring me some sweet little storm.

It's been quite a while since we've heard much about the famous woman pilot, Amelia Earhart. She was officially declared dead back in 1939, so nobody's really looking anymore. But that may be about to change.

A report from Guam contends that Earhart and Noonan were apprehended by the Japanese, though where they were found has not been made clear. Speaking through a translator, a woman who claims to have been Earhart's caretaker says that the pilot and her navigator were held for over a year in a prisoner-of-war camp. She states that the man died while in captivity, but she isn't sure what became of the woman.

Which island may have held the purported camp has not been ascertained. The only statement directly attributed to this new source is that — quote — a blonde woman was seen on an island near Saipan — end quote.

No doubt, we will learn more as this story unfolds, especially if any supporting evidence should turn up.

But now, a word from our sponsor, Ovaltine.

Found

Found by the wrong navy
searching the wrong sea,
arrested as spies
(no trial to be had)

delivered to an island, not quite
abandoned, not quite
inhabitable, not quite
tolerable.

A bent and elderly woman
delivers my meals (semblance thereof,
rusty-bowled, often with sand)
at unexpected hours, serves
as my only source of news, offers
charades for words.

When I ask about Fred
(raise one arm above my head: yea tall,
rub my chin as a beard)
she tips her head, lifts her brow
with a look of "who can say."

Lost

For now, Bush Flier
the name I give myself,
captive of these scorn-eyed men who stare
at my blonde hair, flick their tongues
to scare me, as if they might crawl beside me
into the filthy nest of my bed,
fit themselves, pressing close.

The rise-and-hiss of crashing waves
has hypnotized me sleepless.
I hear steps approaching when no one is there.

Fitful in handcuffed sleep, I dream
a silver bracelet, painted charms, lost
when I was small: a tiny, ivoried elephant,
a broken heart, and best — an ice cream sundae
topped with sliding chocolate, reddest dot of cherry.

How I parted the lawn for days,
never a trace.

News, unwanted

This morn, as I raised my hand to ask,
my silent keeper shook her head,
looked at her feet, walked away,
left me

a piece of fish, wet and raw
on my sodden rice.

from the dirt yard [1]

days here all the same to me
endless hot or hotter
except for bursts of sudden rain
that break the too-blue skies

shadow from a single tree crosses barbs on wire
marks the day, a rosary of hours,
my bleeding the only calendar,
guide to month's name

from the dirt yard [2]

I have learned to eat with sticks
from a bowl of rice
alive with maggots writhing white on white

vigilant, I watch to see
which grubs the birds prefer, the ones
they squabble over as best

I understand my status here
within the pecking order,
hold my humble place in it,

know, among the weakest chicks,
I count for less
than zero

from the dirt yard [3]

Like me, they are skinny birds,
my comrades in the yard, wearing tattered plumage,
unable to fly.

Shy and skittish, they shelter beneath
any trifling bit of green, chitter
so motley a tongue I pretend
enchanted conversations.

When I point at them, rub my stomach,
lick at my lips, the woman shouts
"ne-ne" and shakes her head, grasping at her throat,
makes a sour face toward the ditch where I shit.

My eyes stay focused downward,
absorb my own fowled square of ground.

from the dirt yard [4]

Given times for exercise, ordered less
by hands on a clock than phases of tropical moon
or passing whims of clouds on the horizon

    for the moment I am free, grateful
    to be moving my unshackled legs.

Jangled by open spaces now, I inch
along the wall, clasp my hands
around myself, a straitjacket of flesh.

Like a sparrow, toes curled tight
grasping a twig in the teeth of wind.

Wanting so to be back in sky
inhaling the breath of stars.

from the dirt yard [5]

one day there will rise
a broken tooth unearthed
rag of hankie gone to dust
scrap of paper with my name

a map that will refute the lies
dit-ditted to the world:
flickering newsreels fed like tinder,
igniting the fuse of war

all I have is stone and dirt
sticks I shape to points
semaphore I devise
with my open hands

one day you will find
a crusted locket, hank of hair
some missing jigsaw puzzle piece
that almost spells Amelia

July 18

More of the crazy visions. As if I am living an alternate life. This time with Fred as part of it, waving his hands as hello or good-bye. So many things I do not understand. At least blessed rains came in the night, rinsing me clean, quenching my swollen tongue. I filled my cap, the cracker tin, my piddle jar from the plane. Held my hands as if for alms. Opened my mouth like a baby bird. Wept as I drank. My lips are blistered and bitten, as if from fever, though maybe just thirst. Spent much of the day in dream-filled sleep, almost surprised when I woke to discover I wasn't in Kansas at Gran's. Along with the rains, a new ridge of land has risen, altering this place I now call Fred's Beach. Not much more than a sandbar, like one after spring floods across the river at home. I used to see boys cast out fishing lines there. How I envied them the openness along their Missouri side. My bank riddled only with caves, too small for the escapades I imagined. So many memories crowding my thoughts. That very first flight, when I knew this would be my life. Mother. Pidge. Donk and Ellie. Egg salad sandwiches with lettuce, crisp and cool.

July 19

I have named the new tidal pool Noonan Lagoon. A few odd-looking creatures scurry around in it, even one with spines poking out in every direction. It looks like something that belongs atop a Christmas tree, would no doubt be better there. It stung where I touched my lips to it, down and out dreadful. I caressed the wound with my tongue for much of the day. This eased it some, but there is still a terrible swelling. Lucky thing I don't have to make any speeches tonight. Better comfort was the reddish weed resembling wrinkled cabbage. Salty but no bad reaction so far. If there is more tomorrow, I will try it again.

July 20

The prickly thing was there in plenitude. Out of desperation, I poked at one, moved it onto the sand, smashed it with a rock. Inside was a gooey bit, surprisingly good. Hollow as I am these days, I ate three, hoping for no ill effects. I am so much less mobile than before, tethered to earth with this oversize ankle, my leg like some blown-up lead balloon. Maybe it will rain at least, as thunder is grumbling at me. I have learned to welcome its throaty growl and sometimes pretend it to be the rumble of an engine, a golden seaplane about to alight on the waves and take me home. I can't be sure, but the moon seems to rise higher in the sky. Perhaps I have lost a day. At least there is still a handful of pills. Perchance to sleep, to dream. Afloat in my sea of troubles. Alone.

July 21

Inside me today I felt the flutter of life. Just like that time so long ago, after I'd been in Toronto. It's not indigestion, this feeling is one I remember. Little fish, I bet you sprouted from this spring's Easter treats. But oh, the confusion I feel as you swim inside all a-swirl. Who might you belong to, GP? Or maybe Vidal? Or perhaps to no man. Only to me. Another solo flight to embark upon.

Christmas mornings, juicy hands

The toe of the stocking, heavy and round
its cargo the single orange. What precision required
to pull back the acidy skin,

reveal the net of whitened string
encircling that spicy-sweet globe,
its fingers of such hopeful longitudes.

So much reliant
on the peel in one piece.
Worlds have depended on less.

Declassified inventory item, warehouse 46-756

One piece luggage, 18½" x 14" x 6½," brass clasps, beige satin-lined. Address tag bears name "Me," no street address, only city — Baltimore.

Contents: pair of women's dress pumps, brown leather, low heel; gray cashmere sweater, pullover, with detachable collar; grooming kit (toothbrush, tin of tooth powder, nail file, comb, bobby pins); assorted ladies' undergarments; leather-bound notebook with writings; heart-shaped locket (photos inside, unidentified man and woman).

(Re)Assignment

I have been granted
a husband and son.
This pair of odd strangers,
fabrication to shield me,
sheer as bridal organza.

A cloak of false family
to stand behind
in silence,
playing at being
someone I am not.

My mission: To love

A weak thing, the five-year-old son
pale as poached sole on a white dinner plate,
same age my own little fish would be.

Sometimes the boy stares
at invisible things on air.
As a child, I too was probably such a dreamer.

But my, how I wish he would stiffen his back,
not cry when I push him
too high on the swing.

When I gave him waxed paper
to speed his descent
on the metal slide at the park

my delight, as he flew down,
vanished when he shrieked and wept,
clutching his bleeding knees.

The boy

A feeble creature, this mouth-breather,
who cringes at the mention of going outdoors,
departing the confines of the house.

A line of spittle sometimes drizzles
its string onto his chest,
darkening the patterned cloth
(the same shirt I have burned
precious minutes ironing).

He seems to want only to sit near the fire
arranging his metal collection: painted roadsters,
transport trucks, motorbikes with rubber wheels,
manage them into lines of orderly traffic.
Not so much as a "vroom-vroom" from him,
he's content with mute intersections,
no jangling crashes, crossed connections.

I contrast how Pidge and I used to cavort,
built our curvy roller coaster in the backyard,
splicing salvaged boards to a rickety frame,
then flying across the garden, wild lilies of invention.

Observing his wary ways,
I ask what kind of boy this is,
what child can possibly fear the sky?

Druid Hill Park

Today I forgot myself
helped a stranger fly a kite.

He'd been running with his little girl
skirting the lake along with the breeze
cursing as the paper bird
refused to lift on its spiraling cord.

"Into the wind," I shouted,
pointing as I ran
into the sweetness of moving air
riffling against my cheek.

He held my eyes a bit too long
as if he might have glimpsed
the person inside the decorous pose
I must hide behind. It seemed he almost
said the name, the one I no longer may use.

Moments later, looking back, I saw the glow of his face,
grinning toward the kite
dancing freely, high in the sky,

and I thought of Kitty Hawk,
Orville so courageous, rising from the beach,
flying his rough machine, barely more to it
than a box kite with an engine:
the freedom he understood
if only briefly.

This, my new husband

The father sells shoes, shiny as the pomade
he slicks into his thinning hair.
This dull groom of mine welcomes the war,
explains to me, as if to a child,
"An army marches on its feet."
What am I to learn from this?
Surely, the measuring of feet cannot
fill the needs of his mind.

I would stand with the women
in the factory, if I could.
But no, I am cautioned:
I might show my hand, reveal
some bold trait, one that could draw
unwanted attention. Or worse,

speak out with too strong a thought
one not befitting this pretty head I now wear,
maybe get sent to the loony bin
along with the other hysterical wives,
the ones who didn't behave.

Hair this long annoys me, tangling in the brush,
this continual dyeing of roots to keep them brown,
mouse enough to blend with this dun-colored world
the sentence I must serve, rest of my too-lifeless days.

Oh, for a pinch of danger, a taste of sudden intrigue,
anything to fire up my engines.

Choices

A man in a fedora lingers nearby
whenever I step from the house.

Tomorrow I will fall at his feet
beg to be taken away.

July 22

Once I had an aeroplane
sometimes used to take the train
Do I want to be insane
or do I want to be in pain
Answers plain
as weathervanes
whirling in the rain
Fain that I should be so vain
Do I want to be insane or
do I want to be in pain
in pain in sane
inane in vain
no pain
no pain
no pain

WORKERS HIT PAY DIRT

Workers discovered several items of interest during clean-up operations at the old County Asylum. Most exciting of these finds is a small hand-bound notebook that appears to have the name Amelia Earhart inscribed in it. Although the pages are damaged, the sheaf of notes was taken to nearby Seton Hall University for further examination.

Despite pleas from heritage groups who wished to preserve at least the Administration Center, buildings on the site had fallen into a state of severe disrepair, making demolition necessary. The many hazardous materials, including asbestos, made removal of debris a difficult task, with much of the sorting needing to be done by hand.

The long-abandoned buildings also revealed a number of tiny wooden sculptures that may have been carved by one of the inmates. The investigation continues.

Asylum Blues

I have learned to hide
the bitter taste of broken colors

inside the pouch of my cheek.
I am sorely practiced

can hold my eyes in shadow
half-closed as if nearly asleep,

convince the nurses I have swallowed
their paralytic dosings,

show which face I have selected,
the mask I will wear today:

a downcast one for afternoon
perhaps if it is raining

yet another countenance,
paler if it snows.

Joan of Arc lives down the hall

Wearing her pilled gray sweater
she's armed against the world,
pulling its stretched-out collar up
over her face, protection.

She whispers clever messages
speaks French to her Dauphin,
defends herself with a dented cafeteria tray,
drags a broken clothes tree
proclaims it as her cross.

Now and then she simpers, her armour
getting rusty. I have learned to translate:
she's pissed herself again.

Everyone hoards matches here
even in the rain.

Hallelujah Cavalcade

Lying on this lumpy bed, I invent bold scenes
gauzy-gowned angels slinky enough
to pass through window grills.

One of the seraphim halts mid-air,
unfastens the tip of his wing, leaves a feather
tucked in the furl of my curtain.

A fat cherub trumpets a Harry James tune
its brassy notes flash golden,
echo down and down these yellowing halls.

I can picture a horde of these beings
waltzing me out as I ride, suspended
just above the rise of their wingéd shoulders.

I wear silken slippers,
small and pink as roses.

Yet another winter

Curlicues of snow begin,
swirl beyond the fogged-up glass

smaller than the lacy cloth
knotted in my pocket

hankie with the letter A
embroidered in the corner.

I stitched it there so carefully
its whorls a souvenir

reminding me of who I was,
the plucky girl I used to be.

Snowflakes settle into squared
patches on the gable,

flags of torn white handkerchiefs
flapping in the wind.

Do you read me?

Am.
I am.
I am me.
I am Amelia.

Ear.
Listen ear.
Listen to my wobbling heart.

Air.
Fly on air.
Fly on air like rampant hart.

Fly.
Try to fly.
Trying hard to fly and lift.
Fly and lift a ruined heart.

Listen.
I am me.
Hear me with your ear.

Listen.
I am me.
Listen with your heart.

Listen.
Hear me.
I am me.
Heart in air, Amelia.

July 23

Pain sinks its teeth into my bones, jagged as shards of glass. No more pills to ease the hurt, ward off my maddened cravings. I suck on crackery dust from my pocket, linty succour, a desperate dessert. Tomorrow I must replenish this dry and crumbling stock, fill my pockets, and maybe my mouth, with stones.

True blue

Now that Fred is emptied
of blood and water and soul
all I can do is wait.

No point scanning the skies, I know
they never meant to find us,
their anthem so proudly hailed, now broken.

Even the visiting birds have forsaken me,
as if no longer willing to bear with me.
Still, by gum, I sing to the breeze:

"One of these mornings,
I'm going to rise up shinin'
spread my wings and take to the sky."

Dear little fish of mine, hello.

I think my end is near. O my darling, I am sorry to say, but the end of me shall mean an end to you.

For now, I will pretend that you are sitting on my lap and tell you a story from when I was a girl. It's about two people named Baucis and Philomon, names that I suppose sound terribly old-fashioned. They were poor and elderly, and they lived in a tiny but tidy cottage.

One day two men in rags knocked at their door, begging for something to eat. The old couple invited them in and shared their meager supper. But, the two men turned out to be ancient gods who'd flown to earth, and they asked the pair what reward they might want for their generosity. All they wanted, they said, was to be together always. The gods assured them that they would have their wish.

Years went by, until one summer morning, Philomon and Baucis were working in their garden. Both of them felt their feet forging roots into the earth. And when they looked up and into each other's eyes, they saw that their arms were turning into entwining branches. That's why, when I was a girl, I named two trees outside my grandparents' house after the two of them.

Let's you and I be another Baucis and Philomon and come back some day, together.

You'll always be my favorite fish in the sea,

forever,

your mother

July 24

Tonight will be the fullest moon. Also my birthday, a milestone. I'm not sure whether that fellow who wrote the book was right when he said life begins at forty. How old must he be by now? Is his life still full of beginnings? As for me, this will be the day of my ending. One decision I can make alone, one thing I can do for myself. Too long here, too tired to carry on, too sick, too done.

Send-off, happy landings

This shattered foot hangs from my leg, glum
as a sodden log. A dreaded line of reddened vein
tells me I am a goner, gone gone.

No longer squinting for planes, I seek
only the solace of rain
its coolness to caress my sunburned face.

Those penny-bets I made with Pidge:
how long till the drench of a summer storm
would open the Kansas sky,
soak through our clothes to skin,
making our Grandmother Otis (so prim)
holler us back inside, "Don't you girls even know enough
to come in out of the rain!"

An image of Pidge, long bangs a-stream
over her eyes, makes me laugh.
But then my swelled lips split again, bleed
a salty drink into my weather-torn mouth.

I curse these tides at the planet's waist,
each day's distance farther to crawl.
How many hours to haul myself
to the deeps at the shelf of the reef.

I pray that evening's waves, their slowly lapping tongues
will carry me over the coral to sea, sweeping me free,
will whisper my name to the fishes below, tell them
to leave behind nothing but bones.

Letters on torn pages, tucked into her logbook randomly, are gathered here.

My dearest darling Eleanor, bosomest buddy of mine,

Truly you, my lonely one, must be the one for me. The one who understands the harsh glare of the spotlight, who "gets" me, quirks and all, yet doesn't complain when I whine. So many treasured memories — sneaking off to fly in my little plane, plucking feathers from your boa, tossing them out the cockpit vent so we could make snow.

Let's hope it won't be long when all of us women can toss out our makeup, be whatever we want when we grow up (shucks, do we hafta do that?). A time when we can take off our gowns and fly high as we can aim.

Remember always how I have loved you, sweetest friend.

A.

Dear Franklin,

Thank you for inviting me to all those delightful gatherings at the White House. Always a treat to be in such fine company! I never would have expected that Harpo fellow to be so brainy. How terrible of me, taking him for nothing more than a silly clown.

I do hope sincerely that you will be able to follow your intentions of keeping us out of any new war. The building projects you have established across the country should do much to get the economy rolling — and really, isn't a poor economy always the biggest excuse for war?

I am grateful to have been able to count you among my friends.

Fondly,

Amelia

Dearest Father of mine,

There's going to be a wed-ding! Can you hear the bells? Please come so you can walk with me on the isle. Oh, and a million thankews for the shotgun when I was nine, perfect for this so-shell occasion.

As ever,

Lovin' kisses,

Your doter,

Millie

P.S. I will be the one in bridle attire, being led off to be altared.

My dearest Pidge, cherished sister,

You alone have kept secure the deepest of my private thoughts, just as you have since we were girls, curled in the big bed at Grandmother Otis' house, whispering to each other before we fell asleep. You know my cock-eyed reasons for taking on this loop-the-loop challenge, flying around the middle of the world.

Some of those secrets are probably too sensitive to reveal, at least for now. I ask only that you exercise your always-good judgment. I leave it to you to decide which mysteries to share. Know that I (wherever I may be) shall understand, whatever you do. All I hope is that you hold these confidences close to your heart until such a time when you deem them worthy of revealing.

Please, when you need to, treat yourself and sell some of the skeletons from my closet. Just be sure to fetch a good price, one that may even seem exorbitant to you. Help our sweet mother, but use such monies to live your own life in comfort. And please don't share too much of it with that rascally man of yours. His habits have already nearly proven to be your undoing.

You alone know of my lovers. Kindly see that none of them be subjected to public scorn. This could mean you might need to make up a few tiny lies. When I am gone, your voice must serve as mine.

I will be most grateful if you can deliver some token of my love (perhaps that string of pearls) to the daughter I gave up after my misadventures in Toronto. I believe she is still near the city with the name of our favorite magical bird, the one who flies up from the fire.

I suspect I will not be so fortunate this time as to fly up from any such pyre. I shall love you always, sweet sister.

Yours,

Meelie

xxx

My dear man, GP,

Thank you for tolerating this crazy life with me. You know, I never wanted to be famous. I only wanted to fly. Silly me, to think I could have one without the other.

This is one adventure from which I shall not be coming home. And to think, it was supposed to be my last grand flight! There will be many rumors, some of which will sound like tall tales. Know that some of them are likely true.

Ours was surely an oddball love. I did not mean to fail you, though I am sure I did. Sadly, I also seem to have failed myself.

aep

Among guests at yesterday's gala White House luncheon was Atchison's favorite daughter, our own dear Kansan, Amelia Earhart. She was overheard in conversation with none other than the renowned physicist, Albert Einstein. When she praised him for his achievements, he responded by saying she had made greater contributions for the common good with all she has done to advance the cause of women. High praise from one of the world's greatest men. Yep, that's our gal!

Postscript: Fragment of a recorded conversation (Zurich, 1941)

Male: Ah, Frau Earhart. Und Kind. Eine Tochter.
Female: Ja. Das ist Ella. Muriella. Say hello to the man, darling.
Young child: H'lo.
Male: Willkommen im Institut.
Female: Danke.
[Sound of footsteps receding into distance.]

Amelia Earhart got in her plane
took off from a village called Lae.
Where she went to nobody knows
or else they're not gonna say.

Acknowledgements

Versions of some of these poems appeared in *A: The Amelia Poems*, a chapbook published by Lipstick Press in 2009. I extend gratitude to publisher Janet Vickers for her faith in the writing.

Similar gratitude goes to Vici Johnstone, willing to take a chance on an incomplete and unproven piece of work.

Thanks as well to my hard-working editor, Marion Quednau, who took me by the rudder and steered me in some wonderful directions.

Further, I thank the generous members of my writing group, the Memoiristas, who have supported the concept of this manuscript over the course of its slow birthing. Gratitude also goes to the Chicks, who have stood by me and cheered me on since 1998. Special thanks to Anne McDonald, who ensured the trip to Harbour Grace happened by accompanying me most of the way.

Acknowledgements must also include the American playwright Arthur Kopit, whose one-act play *Chamber Music* no doubt played a role in inspiring the asylum suite of poems.

My gratitude also goes to the staff of the Amelia Earhart Birthplace Museum in Atchison, Kansas. Over the years they have welcomed me into their midst, sharing materials, stories and familial warmth.

And of course, thanks to my family, especially my sister Lisa who has always believed in me, but most of all to George, my co-pilot and navigator who does so much to keep me on course.

About the Author

HEIDI GRECO is a longtime resident of Surrey, BC. In addition to writing and editing, she often leads workshops — on topics that range from ekphrastic poetry to chapbook making. She's been an advocate for the literary arts in her community and was instrumental in establishing two distinct reading series, but she considers her greatest success to have been convincing her city to hire an official Poet Laureate. She writes in many genres — with poems, fiction, essays and book reviews to her credit. Her books include a novella, *Shrinking Violets*, which was co-winner of the Ken Klonsky Award in 2011. Her work has also appeared in many anthologies, most recently in *Make it True: Poetry from Cascadia* (Leaf Press, 2015) and *The Revolving City: 51 Poems and the Stories Behind Them* (Anvil, 2015). In addition to making Sunday suppers for her adult sons, she keeps a sporadic blog at outonthebiglimb.blogspot.ca.

Cover Artist and Statement

LINDA GASS is an environmental artist whose work is informed by nature, maps and aerial photography. She works primarily in textiles, a medium she learned to love as a child when her grandmother taught her to sew and embroider. After leaving a decade-long career in the software industry, Linda began making her unique stitched paintings on silk. She also works in land art installation and glass. She exhibits her work internationally, recently at the Oakland Museum and the US Embassy in Moscow. Her work is widely published in books and magazines. Linda is a native Californian and has lived in the Bay Area for over thirty years.

STATEMENT ABOUT THE ARTWORK: I am inspired by the connections between humans and the water and land that sustain them. In my work, I visually juxtapose vulnerability and resilience, past memory and future possibilities. Growing up in Los Angeles during the drought years made me aware of the preciousness of water, and that realization has turned into a passion for incorporating water-related concerns into my art. I'm drawn to the bird's-eye view of the landscape and the human marks and patterns that are revealed by this view. My study of these marks leads to questions about their environmental impact, which in turn informs my artwork. The aesthetic of beauty is important in my work; it helps make the serious and difficult nature of the subject matter I'm addressing more approachable.

"After the Gold Rush" shows a landscape in California with Interstate-5, a major transportation artery, crossing the California Aqueduct, the man-made river that moves water from north to south and irrigates farm fields in what once was a desert. This is the second mining of California and hence the name of the artwork. (Inspired by a photograph by Ray Atkeson, courtesy of the Ray Atkeson Image Archive.)